THE

Tom Paulin was born in]
and was educated at the ι
He has published five other volumes of poetry as well as a *Selected Poems 1972–1990*, two major anthologies, versions of Greek drama, and several critical works, including *The Day-Star of Liberty: William Hazlitt's Radical Style*. Well known for his appearances on the BBC's *Late Review*, he is also the G. M. Young Lecturer in English at Hertford College, Oxford.

The Wind Dog

TOM PAULIN

faber and faber

First published in 1999
by Faber and Faber Limited
3 Queen Square London WC1N 3AU

Photoset by Wilmaset Ltd, Wirral
Printed in England by MPG Books Limited,
Victoria Square, Bodmin, Cornwall

© Tom Paulin, 1999

Tom Paulin is hereby identified as author of this
work in accordance with Section 77 of the Copyright,
Designs and Patents Act 1988

A CIP record for this book
is available from the British Library
ISBN 0-571-20168-7

2 4 6 8 10 9 7 5 3 1

For Seamus and Marie Heaney

Acknowledgements

Some of these poems have appeared in: *Irish Times*, *London Review of Books*, *The Observer*, *Oxford Poetry*, *Poetry Chicago*, *Poetry Review*, *Princeton Library Quarterly*, *Radio Ulster*, *Times Literary Supplement*. 'My Skelf' was first published in *A Parcel of Poems for Ted Hughes on His 65th Birthday*. 'The Wind Dog' was commissioned by Tim Dee as one of a series of radio poems in celebration of the 50th anniversary of the founding of Radio Three. 'Sarum's Prize' was commissioned by the Salisbury Festival as part of the celebrations of the 700th anniversary of the building of Salisbury Cathedral. 'Sentence Sound' was first published in *Or Volge L'Anno at the Year's Turning: An Anthology of Irish Poets Responding to Leopardi*.

Contents

My Problem

A wall made of air
a wall that's like pure skreeky styrofoam
– of course I'm kidding myself
into believing there must be some
way that with a certain – no not native flair
I can push out and off
till I gouge
scramble scuff
over that jagged – jagged and abstract
wall a wall that's so huge
I can't neglect it
as I sit or situate myself
on the flat land
below a dike outside Delft
where I fidget with the palm of my right hand
in the which
there's this wee skelf
that might just be the jag the gouge the problem

Stile

Close under the eaves of the stack, and as yet barely visible, was the red tyrant that the women had come to serve – a timber-framed construction, with wheels and straps appertaining – the threshing-machine which, whilst it was going, kept up a despotic demand upon the endurance of their muscles and nerves.

Thomas Hardy, *Tess of the D'Urbervilles*

Gaucherie was Gauguin's term
for the style he was after
he gazed on it like Narcissus
till it owned his own features
– try find it though in a printed text
and the sentences gawky or a tad misshapen
– spelt wrong or babu even
tend to provoke laughter
because most critics they're vexed
by what's clumsy or naïf
it must never happen
that something other than platonic form
or hammered gold or pure gold leaf
– that gold to airy thinness bate
should touch us or should warm
the playful serious wondering great
mischeevious child in most of us
– I mean take that word *appertaining*
so dogged doltish so pedantic
a plodsome term – completely daft –
that makes a fuss
and yet in its exact legal decorum
is like a constable who tries to sing

and gets away with it
not murder
for to be clumsy in one light is to be deft
even graceful – graceful not slick –
in another

Kingstown St Vincent

– piece of paper that's been wet then dried
it's a different texture – rougher
a bit like a voice from the other side
or the ricochet of a chough's
cry or the way a voice might move
from *lettuce* to *rocket*
– still a green leaf but peppery tougher

I feel it folded in my pocket
and know it's dull – dull and stained –
that I've written your address on it
and that more much much more is giving me pain
– just touching it is like finding a letter – a love
or a personal letter blowing down the street
so that it feels used dirty torn open
like a cross between a bus ticket's
square of grey print and an unfinished sonnet

Chagall in Ireland

for Roy and Aisling Foster

My childhood *shtetl*
– a mourner slumps down the main street
of this tiny settle-
ment as a halfbrick bursts through my window
while the undented kettle
grows warm on the kosangas stove
like a cat in a basket
– a creaky cricky basket
with a scrap of hairy blanket
that smells of peat
and peat too is hairy
– undaunted the great drayhorse at the forge
turns her luminous eyes
on the nasty fellow
– he's a bad baste –
running down the boreen
where bats will taste flies in the twilight
– asked what'll happen
the march in the next townland
a woman shakes out her apron
oh the night she says
the night will tell the tale
for a moment it's dark and *lumpen*
sort of *Yellow Pages*
but *bather bather* the smith fettles
four metal shoes
for the horse that's glossy and spruce and brown
as ale

5

and the hill above
– hill with a rath
seems somehow engorged
with what? – I
don't want to say blood
but there is for definite metal
– metal and rust – in the image
and we all know how rust tastes
– tastes like sick
or dried shite
and how it's the colour of the culprit's jacket
– see he's got a stick
in his hand now
– the kettle's plumping
I must turn the gas off
he's skulking in the shadows
waiting for me to come down the path
so he can trip this curlyhaired visitor in the mud
but I'll make him and his stick and his brick
shtick
and like someone signing a letter *with love*
I'll paint him into the far corner

The Quinn Brothers

Like those little white boxes
each with a moist square
of weddingcake
but bigger much bigger
or like the watering trough
in Chagall's *L'Auge*
– how the peasant woman bends over it
so tenderly
just as if it's a cradle
– oh not a cradle
a tiny coffin
which means that droll
distrustful green pig
might be death
but death ashamed of itself
as we are whose eyes
catch the green pig's eye
– an eye that looks backwards
to a council house's
orange flames
as they flex up and beyond
the feathery fabulous
powerless tree

Bournemouth

after Verlaine

The fir trees twist down as far as the shore
– a narrow wood of firs, laurels, pines.
Disguised as a village, the town hides out
in these evergreens – red brick chalets,
then the white villas of the bathing stations.

The inky wood drops down from a heath, a plateau;
comes, goes, scoops out a small valley, then climbs,
    greenblack,
before turning into douce groves that hold the light –
it lays gold on the dark, sleepylooking graveyard
which slopes in steeped stages, laidback, insouciant.

To the left a heavy tower – it has no spire –
squats above the church that's hidden by the trees.
That hard basic tower, the wooden jetty in the distance,
are Anglicanism – brisk, bossy, heartless,
and utterly without hope.

It's the kind of moment I like best
– neither mist nor sunshine, but the sun guessed
from the dissolving mist that melts like a dancer,
as the creamy sky turns pink before it goes.
The air gleams like a pearl, the sea's gold, pure gold.

The protestant tower brangs out a single note,
then two three four, then a batch of eight
pealing out like floating feathers.
Eager, joyous, sad, reproachful,
the metal music's gold, then bronze, then fire.

Huge but so mild, it coats the narrow wood,
this beautiful sound that travels slowly
over the sea – the sea appears to sing and tremble
the way a road dings and thuds under the boots
of a battalion marching towards the front.

The sound poem's over. But the madder light
drops onto the sea in thick gobbets like sobs
– a cold sunset, another New Year,
a bloodstained town that quivers there in the west
and wears the darkness like a skewed crown.

The evening digs in, icecold, the slatted jetty
vibrates, and the wind in the wood lashes out
and sings as it whips – a cascade of blows
like the hammerbrash of all I've done wrong
– my sins, my betrayals, the people I've hurt.

I'm heartsick, lonely, my soul's a void.
The sea and the winter winds fight it out.
Like a bankrupt actor, I shout out old lines
and turn the night into ambush, catastrophe,
a smell of greasepaint and cheap evil.

Three chimes now, like three notes on a flute.
Three more! three more! it's the Angelus
out of catholic England that says: Peace now,
the Word is made flesh so your sins can be forgiven,
a virgin's womb has quickened, the world is free.

So God speaks through the voice of *His* chapel
– it's halfway up the hill, on the edge of the wood.
Mother Church, Rome, a cry, a gesture,
that calls me back to that one happiness
and makes the rebel bow before the Cross and listen.

The night strokes me, the forgotten jetty
falls silent under the mounting tide.
Luckily there's a straight track marked out
that'll take me home – like a child I hurry
through a wood that's as dark and scary as the Black Forest.

Sentence Sound

after Leopardi

When I was young – about fifteen or so –
five or six pages in a Fontana paperback
on how the ear
is the only true reader
the only true writer
took me into that uncurtained attic
dedicated to the muse
– here poems are often put together
out of fricatives labials and peachy vowels
here prose is stretched or polished
so it doesn't try imitate
the clearness of that blank windowpane
– and because I was taken to this attic
I admired the workbench its wood
all thick and pitted used but sort of raw
like a floor joist or a railway sleeper
– I admired too
the drills gimlets bradawls hammers punches
even though in more than an hour's searching
I couldn't find a single file
– I searched and searched
missing the raspy texture of the thing
until I lifted a long metal tongue
worn quite smooth out of the wastebin
– I licked – no lisped – that smooth file
till it tasted like either hand of a stopped clock

Man Walking the Stairs

— but the stairs are outside in a stormy garden
where they seem as wild and as bent as the trees
trees Van Gogh or Kokoschka would've recognized
which isn't to say it's at all a secondhand garden
only these trees are ecstatic dionysiac deeply unsettled
oily and ochre and deadened raw yellowgreen
— dingy deliberately dingy is the look and texture they have
— remember Faulkner's *The Wild Palms*? well
these are wild poplars or beeches or chestnuts — but
maybe the poplar that rubbery tree is most likely?
and from poplar to populace is only a short step
so the crowd or the mob have elbowed their way in
which turns all those swirls into street action dustups
which isn't perhaps as farfetched as you might think
for as Canetti points out the crowd has many symbols
— fire the sea rain rivers forests corn wind sandheaps and
    treasure
so the trees are flames that'll either attract a crowd
or represent already the crowd they attract
which means that the cobbled foamfleece in Hopkins's
    Wreck
is a street or a square where halfbricks cobbles bottles and
    stones
as well as petrol bombs and metal bolts are flying
for Hopkins attended monster meetings in Phoenix Park
and knew a fellow priest who'd watched the Communards
rise up like the rooks in Rimbaud's *Les Corbeaux*
— that *armée étrange aux cris sévères*
but if the trees are a crowd in action

why are these steps called stairs?
maybe *l'escalier* means inside/outside?
maybe it means both? and why
is it *man walking* which I read first as *man climbing*?
I suppose in both cases it's just a mistranslation
– *Man Walking the Stairs* is definitely odd
the *ting tang tonk tunk* of two slightly wrong notes
– like *do a tobacco* for *faire un tabac* that is *have a hit*
or *I you ask* for *je vous en prie*
but because I'm in the National Gallery in Merrion Square
I've no means of knowing till I get back home
and check it in the book on Soutine that my pal Jamie has
– book? well the huge *Catalogue Raisonné*
maybe then I'll find out
if it's the climbing – the walking man's back
and his face I can see
and if he's coming or going over
what might be a bridge or an airbright thoroughfare
crossing a stream or a pond
– maybe a pontifex or pontoon
but whatever it is it makes me uneasy
because this stormtossed this in a way nautical garden
has such a closedin such a claustrophobic feeling
and the climbing man is hunched or contorted in some way
– has he his hands tied behind his back like a prisoner?
so he may be taking a last look over his shoulder?
– it could be the Bridge of Sighs then
transposed to nature?
though of course a garden is more than nature
just as the Bridge of Sighs is more than a stone opera
just as the man climbing the steps or the stairs
is more than a man climbing
in the year nineteen hundred and twentytwo

– like a prisoner or a refugee
this man's been told – *walk*!
and everything – stormy trees oily shapes colours
everything in the painting is unhappy
is coerced or coercive
except within it the spirit of the painter
that represents the man
almost as though he's the Wandering Jew
who has been ordered to act the part of a felon
desperately treading a treadmill in a circus tent
that a big wind has blown into rips and tatters

Drumcree Three

On the day of Drumcree
I took an old pair of red stepladders
out of the garden shed
and set them by a wall
where there's an overgrown vine
– overgrown and unkempt
because the poor plant
faces more or less west
and just as I almost never garden
so its grapes stay small green and bitter
show more dust
than ripe bunches ever do
and always look a bit dead

I climbed the tall
slightly unsteady ladder
and started hackling the vine
all the time careful of a nest
– an abandoned thrush's nest
with three blue eggs
dabbled with olive
– eggs no live
scaldy'd ever crack
they lay there like a line
break that doesn't quite work

as I got stuck into the vine
I could hear on the news
– on the radio news

how the police were hacking a path
through the Garvaghey residents
so that a line
of Orangemen in hundreds
could walk – that is march –
down to the church

I felt tense
tried a phrase from Horace
– it didn't *acris hiems*
make too much sense
and kept working the secateurs
– then we went
to a party in East Hendred
drove home in the dark
like a pair of deserters
and hit the sack with a soft crash

I woke at dawn
and went down to my study
to discover a steep red triangle
still standing on the lawn
outside the window
– standing or parked?
for it's not quite the same thing
and the steps' shade of red
looked more like a dulled madder
in that early light
– light so *frühling* early
it walks
catfooted through curtains
like an idea
– which means that sheer

steep triangle
it might have dropped from the sky
all at once
the way ideas were said to
have fallen on Europe
when Toland was teaching
Irish to Leibniz

or else the ladder
was a Jacob's Ladder
out of a triumphal arch
– DERRY AUGHRIM
the usual NO SURRENDER
a masonic chunk
that had somehow landed
in a garden by the Thames
almost like a set theme
that can't ever
be broken into bits
a kind of dry dream

except the thing looked
more like it had risen out of the earth
or been planted on the grass
like a tiny gantry
or miniature derrick
– the sort you see all over Texas
flexing one arm
as though they were king
of each patch of desert
like a doubly belittled
more recent Ozymandias

– then again it appeared
like a type of cubist
hard metal liberty tree
as I stared at this abstract
rather emptied and formal
opened out object
– object or symbol?
as I looked at this spook
this bloody maddening steel stook
it began in its dumb way
like an opened book
to sing *thing*
thing thing
till almost
– and I stress almost
it looked like a dragon's tooth
that had just popped out of the earth
intil the which it had bin drapped

Marc Chagall, *Over the Town*

Marc and Bella
are flying happily over Vitebsk
– they've shucked off the iron husk
of place
and like two salmon trout
've leapt high above the flood
above war revolutions pogroms
– this is a real a shining good
but if you look closely there's a lout
squatting on the mud
near the fence
– like a Brueghel peasant
he's laying a turd
at the edge of their wedding party
and it isn't hard
to know how serious his face
and his bare bum are
though many a reproduction
mars this famous painting
by omitting not just his arse
but the entire squatting lout
whose absence reminds me
how quite a few
critics of T. S. Eliot
choose
either to forgive or forget
those bits of verse
and one piece

of coldly sinister prose
that're about
his fear and hatred of all Jews

The Wind Dog

I married a tinker's daughter
in the town of Skibbereen
but at last one day she galloped away
with me only shirt in a paper bag
to the shores of Amerikay

Snug as a foot in a moccasin shoe
– never the boot no never the boot
I lay in Huck's canoe
one still night
and heard men talking
– clean every word they spoke
on the ferry landing
like the Mississippi
was a narra crick
you could hear across
plum as a bell
– one man he reckoned
it was near three o'clock
he hoped daylight wouldn't wait
more'n about a week longer
so there I lay a clockaclay
waitin for the time a'day

logs float down the Mississippi
logs float down the Mississippi
but
but
don't let's start

the whole caper or caber
don't let's ever grow up

not to roll out the Logos
– at least at the start
or say in the beginning
was the Word
– not to start with a lingo
with the lingo jingo of beginnings
unsheathed like a sword
stiff and blunt like a phallus
or masonic like a thumb
– not to begin then *arma virumque*
– plush Virgil
but to start with sound
the plumque sound of sense
the bite and the kick of it
– green chilli
kerali
white mooli radish
all crisp and pepper definite
– so my vegetable love did grow
vaster than pumpkins and more slow
for the sound of sense
is what the pretend farmer
– Farmer Frost that is
used call sentence sound
because a sentence he said
was a sound in itself
on which other sounds called words may be strung
which – never not quite iambic though –
is ten syllables that hang together – so

– just so
the way the elephant's child
took seventeen melons
(the green crackly kind)
and said to all his dear families
'Goodbye. I am going to the great
grey-green, greasy Limpopo river,
all set about with fever-trees,
to find out about what the Crocodile has for dinner'
just as Rikki-tikki
– Rikki-tikki-tavi
dates me in a carbon childhood
by this huge swollen river
all along a mill village
– soot bracken and stone
where Mrs Jubb
and Mr Jubb whose leathery right hand
had its thumb missing
– where they lived in a back to back
in a deep warm kitchen with a big kettle
like a pet
lived by the music of that bulgy river
that bulgy bulgy river
wider and deeper and slopping at the bank
ever and always ever and always
all those torn waters turning dark
in maybe October
as though the world itself had become bigger and wilder
than the world itself could ever be
because world is suddener than we fancy it
big with itself
gonflé

the huge and shapeless woman
clad in greenish gauzes
and decked
brow nose ear neck wrist arm waist and ankle
with heavy native jewellery
when she turned
it was like the clashing of copper pots
– even she banged a bangle against the tray
when she lifted it to offer me
one of those green sweetmeats
a vein of the gospel proffer the grub the prog
– you know the cargo cult line
that dirty British coaster
its cheap tin trays
cheap tin trays
that's the music speaks me
sings me
makes me
cheeps me
but it's also the cheapo rings on a curtain pole
the way they clishclash too
– something greasy there
greasy or oily
a mixture of brass and unction
like a skitter of listless syllables
that makes me ask
what am I hearing?
what am I knowing?
as the woman – the jum –
in baggy pants
plumps the cushions back into shape
– again the slickslock of her bangles
those silk cushions

the sigh of Hindi being spoken
spoken and then sung
because it's all surface like Matisse
odalisque Matisse
and I'm a child again
a child that reads and hears
but doesn't understand
– who neither comprehends
this nor that
nor the silk sash my father never wore
before the heavens
before the silksack clouds were filled
with the clashing of swords
before I asked Brian Fearon
how much his bottle of orange
– his *bottulornj* cost?
and he said *thhee dee*

then showed me a little brass
little brass hexagonal
thrupenny bit
in the palm of his catholic hand
so I heard *thhee*
for the very first time
on the half between North
and South Parade
before ever I heard it come back in song
– *thhee black lumps*
outa her wee shap
– *candy apples hard green pears*
kanversation lazengers
which is all beginning
all beginning still

yet if I wanted to put a date
when this naked shivering self
began to puzzle at print sound
spokensound
the wind in the reeds
or a cry in the street
I'd choose that room for a start
the bangles
the curtain rings
– it's my baby tuckoo
tuckoo tuckoo it is
not the tundish
this is echt British
except that's always fake somehow
it's machinery means of production
not a spring well
– the well of Anglish
or the well of Oirish undefiled
for this isn't when
but where it happened
where ice burned
and was but the more ice
and salted was my food and my repose
salted and sobered too by the bird's call
the golden bird who perched
on his golden bough
to sing that ancient salt
is best packing
that all that is mortal of great Plato there
is stuck like chewed gum
in Tess's hair
which happened – as it had to –
before ever I seen those tinned kippers

packed into boxes
on the quayside
in Cullercoats or Whitley Bay
and my great aunt
takes the penny ferry over the Tyne
and my English not my Scots granny
calls me *hinny*
and it feels
– that houyhnhnm whinny
of the northeast coast
almost like love and belonging
so I ask myself
why does Elaine Tweedie
say *tarr* not *tar*?
why do I glance down
at her skirt – yellanblack tartan
skirt – when she says it?
what is it almost touching me
like skin warm skin?
I mean we live in two streets
off the same road
– the Ormeau Road
why should we say it different?
and why does my mother say *modren*
not *modern*?
a modrun nuvel not a modern novel
a *f*anatic not a fanatic
which is a way of saying
this is my mother tongue
the gold torc
second time out
for out of Ireland have we sort of come
to find in a book called *The Hamely Tongue*

that the word jum
means a 'large, unreliable trouble-giving car'
as well – it's the dipstick talking –
as 'a large, lazy and probably none too clean woman'
so did that word – the word *jum* –
bob over the sheugh to Broagh
to the riverbroo
the mudshelf of the bank?
or is it Ulstermade?
would you puzzle me that one?
puzzle me proper
while I'm out after mackerel
in an open boat
– blue blue sky
after a skift of rain
the wet wondrous sky
stretched tight like a bubble

– hey Tammie Jack says
d'you see thon wind dog?
look yonder
– what's a wind dog captain?
– ack a wee broken bitta rainbow
tha's a wind dog

we were neither off Coney Island
nor floating down Cypress
Avenoo
– we were out
in the Gweebarra Bay
so I say to myself *Gweebarra*
and drive westward
leaving the picky saltminers

of Carrickfergus behind
me and that lover
of women and Donegal
– 'ack Louis poor Louis!'
was all Hammond's aunt the bishop's
housekeeper could say at the end
it was too looey late to tape her
she was too far gone
what with age and with drink
hardly a mile to go
before she shleeps
hardly a mile to go
before she shleeps
– there used be such crack in that kitchen
her and the maid
always laughing and yarning the pair of them
and wee Louis in the room above
hearing the brangle of talk
rising through the floorboards

o chitterin chatterin platinum licht
the bow shall be in the clouds
and I will look upon it
to remember the everlasting testament
between God and all that liveth upon earth
whatsoever flesh or faith it be
– they may have turned Tyndale into tinder
but the bow he wrought lives high
in this wet blue sky

hardly a mile to go
through the deep deep snow
as I follow another poet's

long shivering shadow
over the crumping snow
– not the journey out of Essex
nor the journey – yet –
out of Egypt
its chisel chipping stone
this is us walking snow
– its widewhite horizon dazzle
the soft quoof
and near crump of it
under our boots
their leather thin and soft
as moccasins
our feet cauld
– *crump crump crump* we go
like break of day in the trenches
as our breath spoofs
in the frore air
soundlessly collateral
and incompatible

how cauld it is
out on air
for the very first time
but not as gross and crass
as the first studio in Belfast
its acoustic deadness
– every wall and bit of furniture muffled
not a shred of echo –
where a cheery *good day*
or – it's Tyrone Guthrie talking –
a ringing roundelay
fell with a dull thud

into a sterilized blank
so two comedians' backchat
it sounded like one mute
telling dirty stories
to another mute in an undertaker's parlour
— so there was none
— it's almost a daft term
like the name of a flower
— none of that 'recorded ambience'
which means the putting back
of silence between sounds
so in the undertaker's studio
there was none
of the living hum of silence
because silence
isn't the absolute absence of sound
— that's death
the undertaker's parlour
silence is the barm the rise the yeast
— so never let those horny feet protood
just parle parle parle
go eat
banana nut ice cream
in a parlour off Ormeau Avenoo
— it's cauld but
like the battlements
on Elsinore
a nipping and an eager air
— *eager* I suppose as in *aigre*
meaning *vinegary bitter acid*
meaning *keen sharp*
like the blade of a knife
no a knifeblade

– put a spondee boy
place a the anapæst!
this is exposure
the here and the now
where we look round the muddy compound
– walls made of tin
or stone or brick
and soggy with sound
wet sound
where we feel
like sick to death almost
a generation
that has come so far
in darkness and in pain
that has heard the sound
– behold we have no continuing city
of gunfire
down streets and over fields
and rooftops
at the Giant's Ring
Shipquay Street
Divis
the Ormeau and a thousand other
roads and streets and fields
round after round after round
– that has heard the sound
of culvert bomb upon culvert bomb
that plump and heavy sound
that tells us
– master of the still stars
never such innocence again
as it dumps and bumps and crumps
over the snow

near Swordy Well
there's a frozen lane between stone walls
– high stone walls
listen
our nailed boots wi clenching tread rebound
& dithering echo starts and mocks the clamping sound
– all the way
from the acoustic deadness of that studio in Linenhall Street
to the poet who died
in the same asylum as Lucia Joyce
– *Yet what I am none cares or knows*
My friends forsake me like a memory lost
I am the selfconsumer of my woes
– all the way
to a brook in Northamptonshire
Were as one steps its oaken plank
The hollow frozen sounding noise
From flags & sedge beside the bank
The wild ducks brooding peace destroys

walking the plank
we turn the bridge into a thunderbox
– blocks of dead sound
drop *bock bock bock*
into the air
as though something formal and dreadful
is both happening and about to happen
on this wooden platform
– sound is always ahead of itself
– at least sound that has an echo
and a living skin of air
ambient air
around it

so sound is both Being and Becoming
like that river that bulgy river
where I walked with Mrs Jubb
one maybe October evening
in the third or fourth year
of this
my life

Odd Surname

People who write me about my name
– to them I'm grateful
they don't ever say what a nuisance
always to be spelled out name it is

one that comes back as Powlin Pauling
Pauline or Panlin
– the billycan campfire tinniness
of that I like but Pollen's the worst

– as a kid in class – nature study
or geography
I'd roast when two subjects were discussed
– pollination or the freshwater

herring that's found only in Lough Neagh
Pollan its name is
Paulin though's from someplace else – so far
I've put no trace on it but sometimes

out of the blue a letter'll mention
an origin like
Spitalfields – so maybe one day I'll find out
if it's Huguenot or Hugue*not*?

Theta Is Better

Late or lateish in my life
– my life as a failed linguist
I've come to θ
that is I've come to the thuh
in thanatos
and this thuh sound
– that dull basic foreclosed thud
it isn't a happy sound
for θ was the sign
a juror would scratch
– scratch on a potsherd
when he favoured the death sentence
– at least that's what it says
in *Teach Yourself Greek*
so θ
it's near enough like stubbing your toe
– but no not quite
more like a breath stubbed
agin your teeth
or a lapith
kicking a marble centaur
in its teeth
– but the dumb sign
it looks like an egg
with a hair or a line across
or like a mechanical
even an arid plum
(either way it's a zero sum)
or else this hairy line

maybe looks like a krait
like the bootlace snake
that never fails
to take us down down
into the underworld
– so the egg is a daylight god
but the hair
I'll follow it like a trail
that leads to a trial
that leads to a stair
– I'll climb that steep stair
not yet disembowelled
of my natural entrails

three four
knock at the door
– imagine the door as subject
no mystery
just a coathanger
a formal object
on which for some reason
you've to drape its own history
– how it began
– is *began* better than *started*?
– began as the flap on a tent
made out of cloth or hide or felt
like the tent itself
– then the door proper
made of what's termed
rigid permanent material
that came about si-
multaneously with architecture
– various big squat
round or high
buildings whose doors
were made of stone or bronze
and had heavy hinges
whose pivots
were coated in lard or oil
so they didn't scringe
– notice though how among several
definite objects
we've got felt and lard
so on one level
this must've something to do
with Joseph Beuys
a heroic artist like James Joyce

except he's more like Icarus
because the young Beuys – nineteen –
was a Stuka pilot in the Luftwaffe
a prince of the air yes
conscripted by darkness
like Satan
but a no-sayer to the Nazi cause
– unstrapped and unbuckled
he flew into a black smoky clatter
– Soviet ack ack that sounded
like munching apples in church
– his plane bucked and lurched
then crashed hard
into the Caucasus
– young Joseph lay crushed
in the smashed cockpit
– deep snow windhowl emptiness
no search party no one
till a voice said *voda*
and made him sip steelcold water
– two Tartar tribesmen he'd known
back at the airbase
– *Du nix njemcky*
du Tatar
took him into their tent
where they rubbed his body all over
with grease and soft lard
wrapped him in layers of felt
and strapped them tight

in the tent
a dense smell of cheese grease milk
he was out of it for a fortnight

then they strapped him to a sledge
and lugged this felt parcel
to the German lines
– a pissedoff sentry
mangy and frostbitten
in the lichened daylight
pointed to a flap
on the hospital tent
– inside a smell
of disinfectant and crap
but as they lift him into that orderly hell
it's another threshold another liminal
bar another edge
I meant to take as part of this subject
– if it is a subject
for twentyfive years after
Joseph Beuys was lifted
from his wrecked Stuka
and enveloped in felt
I'm reading Heaney's latest book
– *Door into the Dark*
in a bed and breakfast
a creaky Georgian farmhouse
maybe near Limerick
somewhere anyway in the west
– it's so far back
it's like the year nought
and why should the place matter?
why name what patch of ground
now thirty years later?
I've stepped back into the dark
to catch the hammered anvil's shortpitched ring
and to take the stress

of that precise shortpitchedness
how it dings
– stopped short abrupt
how it sting sting stings
like bullets in a tunnel
its thingness
like sparks in your eardrum
part of a pattern
of foreclosed sound
almost as if the bank's stepped in
and put a bar
on any right of redemption
or else that shortpitched ring
might be the underground creak
of the state's static timbers
or again it might be
a type of ontological
split that also heals
– that is anneals
it all back together
like some phantom particle
that both splits and doesn't split
– it's a civil war trope
that maybe cancels hope
or does it?
I couldn't frame that question
– not as a youth not then
but the way the eye bends
to the big black anvil
horned as a unicorn
and square at one end
– this was a door sill
one of the very first

and because reading's a social
always a social act
I began to feel nervous
– there was something inside
that was also outside
something on the loose
– I was ill all that week
– ill with a heavy bronchitis
so when I switched off the light
the darkness of that mouldy bedroom
was too absolute too thick
like the steep essence of night
that can frighten you sick
– I imagined a door
disguised as a bookcase
the eight o'clock walk
to the greased trapdoor
then that hidden chalk
mark on the inside
of Tom Paine's cell door
– it was shut and that saved him
from the death squad in the corridor
– but these are a young skite's
callow fears
I've been here before
and later grown weak and flustered
in front of a blistered door
– the door
of an empty farmhouse
between Ballyiriston and Maas
– inside a stink of damp and disinfectant
on the table – bare table –
one halfempty

bleared bottle of Powers
– only a half bottle
like a kind of subtraction
or like a tomb gift
from the dead to the living
a bottle that didn't imply
any human connection
– it'd never be lifted
to the rim of a glass

outside banal and forever
the blistered paint on that door
was like bladderwrack
ready to be popped
ready to pop off
like the old cattle farmer
who worked a hundred acres
and tried to live on air
– but no turfstack
no beasts in the back
– that poverished field –
no halfdoor like a welcome
in the cottage next the barn

– no harm
but this is losing the plot
because each and every door's
what you beat your head against
– a door is more than a fence
it's complete denial
and even Ghiberti's great bronze doors
the *Porta del Paradiso*
on the Baptistery in Florence

– doors that took twenty years
to shape and cast and hang
– even those enormous doors
overwhelm as objects
as foursquare function
and can never be as pure as song
– they belong to epic
like the grating hinges in Milton
or the crazy door of the jakes
that Bloom kicks open
a jerky scraky shaky
door
that because we ken
a particular pong
– mouldy limewash and stale cobwebs
it's like coming home
and knowing it is home
– and so Bloom came forth
from the gloom into the air

Le Crapaud

after Corbière

An airless night a sort of song
– moon a metal plaque
its tattery shadows inky green
... buried alive under those laurel roots
the song's a slimy echo pulsing pulsing
– he shuts up – look he's down by the drain
– a toad! his pursy skin pubbles
but I'm guarding him with my own skin
– look at him – a wingless poet bald as a coot
a mud nightingale a singing turd
... he starts his song again *yuk yuk yuk*
why'm I disgusted? see the light in his eyes
no – he flubs under some mooncold rubble

*

night night – fat Mr Turd he's me

Oxford

This morning I pass a big clump of purple buddleia
by the river and catch their honeyed scent
and notice again how they're shaped like *kulfi*
– like Indian icecream
then as I walk towards the Bodleian
there's this old man finishing a yellow dream-
like enormous watercolour of the Radcliffe
Camera – perhaps he's a nephew
of Charles Ryder? with that precious nostalgia
which might be all this cavalier place is meant
to mean though take that word *camera*
and you'll find it means *room* in Latin
just as the word *kamra* in Punjabi
also means *room*
so that from the Land of the Five Rivers
to Ancient Rome
to this three hundred year and more dome
is as short and sweet as a piece of *burfi*

Sarum's Prize

'Its spire a poplar or an aspen leaning against the wind,
yet firm as a rock.'

Because the style called Romanes-
que buckles under pressure
– those dull round arches
are dense
like nougatine or fudge
– they never tense
because that style won't budge
English Gothic took the stress
– it simply had to
freeborn noble quirky
its impassioned gestures
burst like water from the water meadows
into something graceful and jerky

spring sprang or sprung rhythm
an entirely new measure
leapt out of that dark backward abysm
– yes the past is always murky
and in its fountainy *virtù*
that new rhythm
– rhythm and jaggy mass
made a permanent surprise
that Master Elias
his builders and his masons chose
as Sarum's prize
but as rough canvas has the right tooth for some
driven desperate painters

or yacking consonants clipe the ears
of riven poets
– clipe or clasp like jism
kicking for the ovum
so Gothic's a style like frett-
y chervil – that is organic
like a salad
even though its mystery and dread
echo that mix of *no* and *yes*
that is the light
– the freakish splintery bursting risky light
rising out of chaos darkness
and old – that is too ancient – night

The English Republic

for David Norbrook and Sharon Achinstein

Lucan whose name's
now nearly forgotten
was a hater of kings
– a classical republican
like Marvell and Milton
yes it almost stings
me he's got the same name
as an Irish icecream
– a boring one
bodged into sliders
an undistinguished spa town
outside Dublin
and that murdering dopey lord
who may be lying doggo
at the bottom of the English Channel
or waiting for Godot
in a palm hut where his argot
makes no sense at all
– so this single word
is a kind of tunnel
away from a wider
daylight theme
– away from the sun
its great Now of light
and into blind night
into messy or trivial things

Chagall Designs Christy Mahon's Costume

The elements and the stars of night
moonlight in a windskiffed puddle
a sealskin waistcoat and a lamp
filled with seal oil
– ah thick thick and fishy the smell of it
when you pour oil down the tundish
as outside the cows're breathing and sighing
in the stillness of the air
its mushy barearsed smell
eighty jugs six cups and a broken one
an ivory penknife three whiskey muddlers
– for why this length of hemp?
two plates and a power of glasses some lump
sugar and a pair of dainty boots
two bone brushes for to stroke her hair
the boner they give me as I flex their bristles
– soon I'll be rinsing out a shining
tumbler for a decent man
I'll tell him – Mr Boyle –
how I passed ten tinkers that were camped
in scabby tents by the fair
and how I saw the soldiers' clean white tents
and heard the sergeant's whistle
too clean too sharp it cut me to the quick
and brought back those two young soldiers
they shot kneeling each on his own coffin
for ministring the United Oath
then that night
I crossed through the Stooks of the Dead Women

and saw the big hump of Inishboffin
– oh she's far from the land
where her young hero sleeps
but I could see them both
those shadows of the living dead
that're like a darker light inside the light
I was naked as an ash tree under a big May moon
as naked as a seal on the White Strand

Craquelure

A term – technical term –
with no allure
– not unctuous not brittle
like pork crackling
so there's the usual question –
why bother?
except it's the germ
– like seeds in a mummy's stomach –
of whatever
for clearly this is an antiquarian
subject that's irredeemably
committed to the letter
and fixed like bone ache
or too clipped a metre
– it's like writing about the worm
in the apple
a worm that's all dry skin
and not pliable
– like choosing that instead of a dippling
branch or its blossom
or four greeny blue eggs in a nest
eggs that'll one day – now I see –
crack open
so I'll turn
to the River Quoile at neap tide
a dusty car rug on the grass
where
each with an easel and a sketchpad
my mother and her friend Kathleen

are painting watercolours
of the diminished river
– a skift of rain
comes so close
it nearly spots their paintings
as swans go skidding and sliding
and splashing along the blue water as they land
and the light and the air
are nutfresh open chittery

the muddy estuary
– mud not sand –
has a dull wet mouldy vegetable smell
like dead soup
or the inside of a cracked downpipe
or a broken drain
– I find a clay more clay than earthen-
ware bottle in the mud
and in the bottom of the bottle
I can make out a dead scaldy
– a fledgling –
or at least think I can
– it's a creature neither invented
nor dreamed up
– just found
and in its being found small
banal and scruffy
on these somehow anal mudflats
but then – I'm ten years of age –
if it can almost terrify
the scaldy mightn't really exist

it mightn't be in this cold nest
which is therefore a bottle with a smell
but no message

Vitebsk

sounds like stubbing your big toe –
no not quite
more like someone smashing
a fence down – it's the crash
of flimsy timber breaking like the laths
in a plaster ceiling as some shite
kicks his hobnail boots
on the edge of your vegetable plot
or up in the roofspace
– yes I paint the folkloric
paint peasants and fiddlers
trees that dance without roots
but any praise of the *volkisch*
it makes me feel sick
– now let him kick at the palings
as they stand in a line
let him know that I'm not
going to die
for a long long time – almost a hundred years
until my very last sigh
– but hold to your doubts
and know before our tears
can drown the wind
or chalk horses can race
in sunshine
through the almondgreen meadows
his children's children
will seed the earth with our sorrows

The Unholy One?

At 10 – let's be specific –
at 10 a.m. you'd be sitting in your deckchair
filling pages with shorthand
so I imagine a caption in the *News Chronicle*
GBS TRAVELS P&O
'I always work on holiday'
says the world's most famous author
'especially if some kind cruise liner pays me'

so there you are on deck in a deckchair
a kind of rational tautology
dry as your deckchair
and like its flat depth
still slightly intriguing
because your plays are engines
each of them equipped with a möbius strip
instead of a fan belt
– they run on ideas
well they're powered by will
and opinions

at 12.45
just before a carrot and celery lunch
you hand the stenographer your notebook
she knocks up a typescript
while you munch and read
– it's as regular as clockwork
this perfection of the plain style
and you're a zinc stylus

a clone of yourself like your characters
– characters one critic
rightly calls statues without shadows
because to design them
is to be a morse pad
in sea or space
in desert or prairie
– we catch the flickering tick of your message
tick tick tick
a cold tickle
not Rikki-tikki
no not quite
– not the *nail* the mongoose
dancing out of a dark
a dark tattery sugarcane grove
– no your tick is more straightforward
has more the tilt
of a skylight
– a skylight deckchair
and though Joan's your Antigone
you wrote more like Creon
– wrote that is for what Hegel
calls the daylight gods
– the gods of free selfconscious
social – social and political – life
the gods if you like
of middleclass conversation
its Fabian certainties
its brisk *of course*
that's often slightly off course
like the old Belfast story
– that overtroped seachestnut
of the liner and the iceberg

– all of which is a way of saying
that your homage to daylight
to *claritas*
means the gods of family tribe the subconscious
aren't your sort of thing
– which is why Yeats
dreamed you were a Sing-
er sewing machine
– so Yeats imagined you
as a smiling machine
both a purring cat
and a fixture
– and then in a letter
rejecting *John Bull's Other Island*
said you had for the first time
'a geographical conscience'
– which means your other island
savoured of the earth
had even the oily tremor of bogland
– I guess he meant to imply
that all the rest
– all your other plays've the buzz
of an early electric razor
that they're talking heads
with stubble on every chin
– really I think your characters
they feed on something like brillo pads
and emit sparks
from their always mobile mouths
while you patrol them
like the solitary warder
in the civic – civic not lonely tower
at the centre of that immense panopticon

called the Shaw Canon
because reading or watching your work
we're addressed first by a tannoy
then we enter
your nearly Bauhaus foyer
– nearly because Beatrice Webb
designed its utility furniture
– we look up
and see a security camera on the ceiling
– that's not fair though
I mean you were the last
person to care about private property
but you watch us
like the panopticon's warder
– I keep wondering
what you would have said to Bentham
or whether you ever talked
to the autoskeleton in its glass cupboard
– that would've been your version
of a Yeatsian séance
– I can see you sending
WB a postcard –
'Chatting to Bentham yesterday:
he told me
quantity of pleasure being equal
Cathleen ni Houlihan
is as good as *Riders to the Sea*.
Yours, GBS.
P.S. I was born in Upper Synge Street.'
– now I think of Iris Murdoch's novels
or those copies of Wisden
sunbaked like yellow biscuits
in Beckett's Paris flat

and then of that late lovely poem
MacNeice's 'Budgie'
where the caged bird with its mirror
is compared to a television
actor admiring himself in the monitor
though to say this
is to sound ungrateful
and that dear GBS
is not what I am
for like Swift you aimed to vex
your audience
– like a mischievous
– a mischeevious boy
you scattered itching powder on your pages
and wrote English
as if it was a form of Esperanto

now I see you
helpless with laughter
as your mother's coffin
bursts
into what you called beautiful fire
then you phone your broker
and tell him to take out shares
in the crematorium
– but I won't leave you there
for like an aertex vest
you keep us warm
in a type of shared
schoolroom intelligence
in you opinions
are as common as onions
– Verlaine's Tennyson

is well Verlaine
compared to you
– you're the most opinionated writer
who ever lived
perhaps what you tread
is that fine distinction
– a kind of knife edge
between theatre and drama
– Boucicault is theatre
ever so fluent theatre
Martin MacDonagh too is theatre
but let me ask this question
– are you ever dramatic?
– that moment in *Heartbreak House*
when Hector Hushabye
alias Marcus Darnley
is reported to have been found
as a baby
in an antique chest
one summer morning in a rose garden
after a night
of the most terrible thunderstorm
– that merely narrated moment
it's a glance at *a handbag!*
in *Earnest*
which in turn is an echo
of the satchel that held
the baby Oedipus
in the crooked pass of Kithairon
– his tiny ankles spiked
his cries like a quail's
– a quail trapped in a net
on Mount Kithairon

– but where does your antique chest take us?
not to blind Oedipus
led by his daughter Antigone
that's the living ginger
fate destiny
the place where three roads meet
but in you the secular
is taken to the absolute limit
so I see you
not so much beating on heaven's gate
as taking a centrebit and brace
and drilling at those gates
and as you drill
another Dubliner
– Mr Leopold Bloom
looks on and approves
because Bloom read you
– he read you in a kind of prolepsis
– I mean he read you
even before you'd published
several texts
so it was rather mean of you
never to finish *Ulysses*
– which means
I should stop gabbing on
and your play should begin

The Emigration of the Poets

after Brecht

Homer belonged nowhere
and Dante he'd to leave home
as for Tu Fu and Li Po
they did a flit through the smoke
– 30 million were no
more in those civil wars
while the high courts
tried stuff Euripides under the floor
and even Shakespeare got a gagging order
as he lay dying in Stratford
– Villon who wrote 'Les Pendus'
had visits from the Muse
and from the Beast
– i.e. the police
though at least Lucretius
was nicknamed *Le bien aimé*
and slipped away from *Heim*
just like Heine
– now watch me here Bertolt Brecht
I'm a pike
shtuck in this Danish thatch

Drumcree Four

The preacher
you know that costive overreacher
the mate of biblebashing lechers
says the Twelfth will be the settling
time then reaches
for his blackthorn
and marches to the barricade
– no more
flicks this time of the Orange Card
– they're in a tribal huff
it is a standoff

I listen to the radio
I read the papers
but how this caper
will end no one knows
only the word *settle*
its clanky its metallic
even archaic sound
hits the ear
like listening to a battered kettle
or a tin can
being kicked across a patch
of rocky ground
or concrete walkway
– should we cut an eyepatch
for the pirate preacher
then snap his stick?
he claims this patch of ground's

his tribe's alone
and through a megaphone
he gulders with a deep thick
ululating wheezing sound
that strains like Ulster
in a bulging holster
that bible uniform
pressed by what his father stuck
to – now watch the British state
as with fairness and no hate
it grasps the nettle
and says – walk? no way

My Skelf

The way you might put a kink
in a fishing line
or happen on the name *Grigson*
– Geoffrey not Jane
(did he write about Ted?
no I haven't a clue)
– or say that *skink*
is a spilling word
with something in it that's irksome
that doesn't pour out fine
and handy
like a length of cord
all loose and easy
and with never a knot
is what I'm trying to trace just now
as I wander among the philosophers
and find that the mind
needn't go A to Bwards
or bind on all the time
as if the only direction is towards
some naff goal
as if there must always be a link
from this to that
with no room ever to tinker
soodle or dander
– no it can be lazy your mind
and thrum on nothing if it so desires
absolutely nothing
– but still it's the crick the grig

in whatever
that's lodged with me like a tick
a thorny wee tick
or a skelf
– it's the way you might bait a fish hook
with a little lump of curd
and ask why ever was I born?
why did I go into that cellar
full of forgotten – forgotten
or surplus – apples
all rotting in the dark?
why was it summer outside
and dark and warm under that thick
concrete ceiling?
– it was thick like a bomb shelter
so why did I find in Jean-Jacques
– in his childhood
the windows were darkened
by raspberry canes?
and why on earth did we shack
up in that rackety house
next the railway line?
– no it didn't work
it didn't work
and now it seems absurd
even a shade ominous
that I should think
I've become one
with the author of *The Confessions*
and in just seven words
can hear a shifting of gears
then a sound that goes
tink tink tink

as though consciousness
must be a tiny tinny twostroke
whose importunate chink
beats like soundtrack
all the way to Madame Guillotine
before *The Battle of Algiers*
has even begun

The Utile as Fetish

That squat red tub of Swarfega
on their bathroom windowsill
ought to be ranked with the household immortals
– each time I come back here it's still
there in the exact same place glum but eager
to leach deep dirt out of masculine palms
– I know this dark liquid's gritty chemical dull
part of what it means to be a real man
doing real work as my father still affects
to do – it belongs to some cargo cul-
ture of grotty scavenged alien objects
even though it's manufactured under licence
in Finglas – it goes with spanners clappedout vans
the diesel the greasy the plain basic but useful

Not Musical

Something in the fiddle's tone
that I can't know I know
– which is only to say
that its sound its slow
strutty glumness 's too thrawn
as I hear in its belly an offcolour
sound like furred echoes in a cellar

and does her bow fray
under not over its yelping stresses?
all I know's the clash
of consonants – their broken jaggy tune
like a chough's call
the way they scrape or scringe or smash
– I have no right to say this
no right to speak at all

Paris Ink Sketch

after Verlaine

Scrubbed like a bartop the roofs look tin
or moony zinc – upended – all angles
like baths and sinks in a plumber's merchants
while out of pointy pencil chimneys
smoke – sinless – scribbles its 5s

the sky's grey – an echo – an encore
like a weepy bassoon
till a stinking tomcat nesh and mangy
screeches strangely
– a cry that's kinked like catgut really

me I walk the streets dreaming of Plato and Phidias
Oedipus and the Sphinx
– those thinking Greeks their forms ideas!
under the blinking eye of these blue gas lamps
these burning beaks

A Naive Risk

des bribes et des morceaux
– the smallscale model
ship in the bottle
odds and ends
so enter the Jack
of all trades who mends
most anything
and can grow
Cos lettuces inside the wooden O
of a Walworth garden
and if from Walworth
with its wooden walls
and video stores
to Wellworths in Strabane
is o-
nly more than a mile or two
as the last bomb in the whole of Ireland
blows the store
up into the heavens
with no one thank God
getting even the slightest bit hurt
reenter the Jack
who takes – you've guessed it –
a lump of churt
from a beach near Dumfries
a strip of cloth
a toerag burnt match
an old tin can
and a business card

– Ruth Moth
Aroma Therapist
so you can catch
something both charred
and annoying as plaque
that might also harden
slowly dare one say it
into art?

July, 1998

?Chesterfield

It's a buckled arrow
pointed like any spire
at the sky above the town
or a leaf that has turned from greenness
to a brittle a crumpled brown
or else it's a cracked bell that rings
its *maudit* mardy tone
every time you look up
and wonder at the dinge
the twist
on the flank
of this oddly angled *flèche*
that balances – just –
like a question mark
over the house of God
and asks *am I loved?*
or *does God exist?*
it might be a broken bone
that's badly set
or a fragment of the dark
even a scream or shriek
like a bat
trapped in the belfry
or maybe a skreeky rhythm that keeps
trying to sort itself out
and get back
– *whatever are you a*
at? –
either to Eden or heaven

some place that doesn't itch
that's perfect and normal
with never a dropped stitch
haitch
missing rhyme or tune

but what's it like to live
with this perpetual scringe
every day of your life
in the same small town?
it's like a child's gawky
drawing a naïf
sketch of the real thing
whose leaflike
look is in fact the real thing
and that's plain awk-
ward another breach in nature
unmistakable grief
or song that –
poor creature –
's dinged
every time the music begins
either that or a squawky
rooster perched above the roofs
its cry a tin can
being kicked all over town

does each citizen
of this almost forgotten
market town
– if that's what it is
– does each citizen cringe
whenever they catch sight

of this rusted hinge
into the Anglican heaven?
or does it hang like a cliff
– fair to say crapulent? –
over their steady lives
a starvation diet
like a permanent Lent
or reminder of sin
those years in the desert?
or do these stoic burghers
simply shrug and say
'appen it's a false note
but catch that homey dissonance
and its bingdring
turns into a grin?

Before Apple-Picking

When Eric Brown placed that bakelite disc
on the turntable
in our pocked aluminum
and hardboard classroom
I was like a boy in some tale
who might – just – be able
to see the danger the risk
in that *long two-pointed ladder*
bobbing against an apple-bough
– he's lost up there in the leaves
like Jack climbing the beanstalk
as right now
he empties his bladder
and watches a streel
of shattery shining piss
bounce off the leaves
like rain or smalltalk
as in the swales
of stormy light
he finds himself in a kitchen
where there are four crocks
charged with new milk
while at the window a mitching
boy – Joe Ward –
dodges out of sight
hugging a strapped cardboard box
on which there's one word
stamped in big block letters

that the stupid messer
swaying amongst the Coxes
completely fails to notice